Glories & Stories

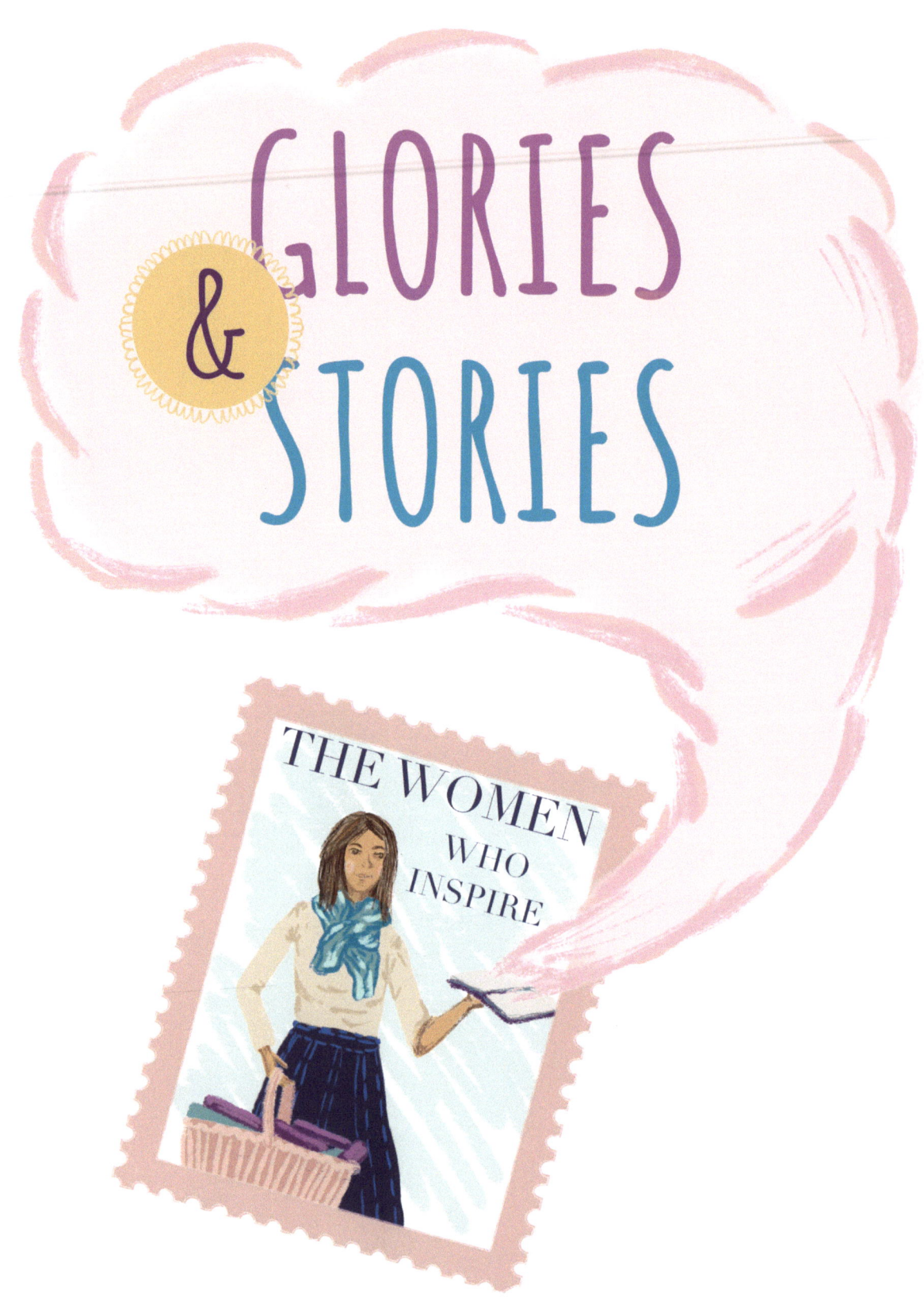

THE WOMEN WHO INSPIRE

Written By Sara Abdelhadi-Bejaoui

Illustrated by Hiba Malik

This book belongs to
_____

To the aspiring leaders and change-makers of the world.

Glories and stories : inspirational American Muslim women
Written by: Sara Abdelhadi-Bejaoui Illustrations by: Hiba Malik

Text and Illustration Copyright @ 2021 by Connected Collectives Publishing

All rights reserved. This book or any portion thereof may not be reproduced or used in any manner whatsoever without the express written permission of the publisher except for use of brief quotations in a book review.

978-1-7368028-2-3 (Hardcover)
978-1-7368028-0-9 (Paperback)
978-1-7368028-1-6 (Ebook)

Publisher's Cataloging-in-Publication data

Names: Abdelhadi-Bejaoui, Sara, author. | Malik, Hiba, illustrator.

Title: Glories and stories : inspirational American Muslim women / written by Sara Abdelhadi-Bejaoui | illustrated by Hiba Malik.

Description: Includes bibliographical references. | Newport Beach, CA: Connected Collectives Publishing, 2021.

Identifiers: LCCN: 2021904779 | ISBN: 978-1-7368028-2-3 (hardcover) | 978-1-7368028-0-9 (paperback) | 978-1-7368028-1-6 (ebook)

Subjects: LCSH Muslims--United States--Biography--Juvenile literature. | Muslim women--United States--Biography--Juvenile literature. | Women in Islam--United States--Juvenile literature. | Women in science--Biography--Juvenile literature. | Women in business--Biography--Juvenile literature. | Women in education--Biography--Juvenile literature. | CYAC Muslim women--United States--Biography. | Women in Islam--United States. | Muslims--United States--Biography. | Women in science--Biography. | Women in business--Biography. | Women in education--Biography. | BISAC BIOGRAPHY & AUTOBIOGRAPHY / Women | BIOGRAPHY & AUTOBIOGRAPHY / Cultural, Ethnic & Regional /General

Classification: LCC BP67.A1 A33 2021 | DDC 297/.082/0973--dc23

For bulk orders contact: info@connectedcollectives.com

Dedication

For my beloved mother, Hajja Om Thaier, and my sisters Nathmia and Shama, who have raised me in becoming a confident Muslim-American woman. To the amazing men in my life, my father, Hajj Abu Thaier and my brothers, Thaier, Abdelmageid, Yahya, Mohammad, and Hamza, who have supported me through every step of the way. To my loving husband, Zied Bejaoui, for believing in me.

Author's Note:

Sara Abdelhadi-Bejaoui is a Palestinian American clinical and school counselor as well as childbirth educator and doula based in Southern California. She holds a M.Ed. in Professional Counseling and a B.A. in English and Sociology. This is her first children's book. Glories & Stories: Inspirational Muslim American Women was written to showcase empowering Muslim-American women and to help motivate the next generation of leading professionals. To write to the author, e-mail info@connectedcollectives.com

As a counselor primarily serving the Muslim-American population and an active member of my community, I recognize the importance of uplifting one another. I take pride in hearing success stories of the courageous and devoted Muslim-American women who greatly contributed to U.S. history. It is my hope that the children reading this book get inspired from some of the exceptional mentors that strive in their professions. May they serve as role models to the young girls and boys from all walks of life. May this book enlighten conversations between children and their parents about their careers and future ventures.

ZARINA ALI

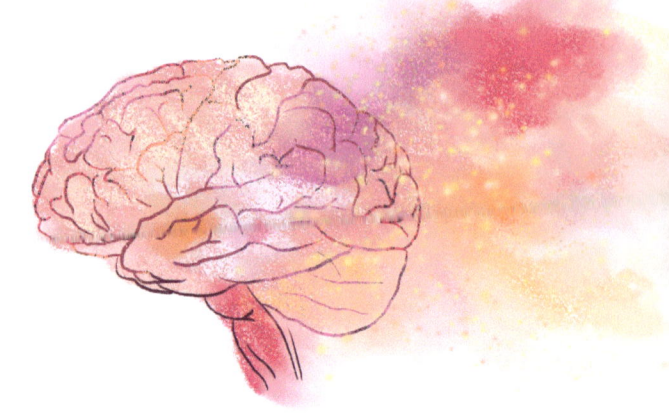

Zarina Ali is a doctor whose studies focus on the body and brain.
Her work has brought the field of science a big gain.

The first female neurosurgeon at the nation's oldest surgical center,
Zarina is known to be an extraordinary mentor.

Her efforts to become a doctor were determined and dedicated,
and she takes pride in the hard work she did to become educated.

IBTIHAJ MUHAMMAD

Ibtihaj Muhammad, known for defense and position,
won a medal for the USA in competition.

The first hijabi woman winning her Olympic sport,
Ibtihaj's Muslim family gives her full support.

Olympic athlete, Ibtihaj has fencing skills, no doubt,
she's proud of her religion. Ibtihaj—a girl devout.

ANOUSHEH ANSARI

Anousheh Ansari is the first Muslim woman to go to space.
Shooting for the stars is what earned her that place!

She started a business that arranged trips to travel beyond Earth
and is known as the first Muslim female to take advantage of its worth.

A successful businesswoman and engineer,
through her hard work and perseverance, she became a pioneer!

NOOR TAGOURI

Noor Tagouri writes with passion and purpose.
Her work brings equal treatment of all people to the surface.

She shares stories from different communities,
inspiring people to reach for better opportunities.

Through all types of media she showcases her voice
and encourages society to make the right choice.

CHARLENE ELDER

The Honorable Charlene Elder is a judge.
She makes decisions without holding a grudge.

Charlene handles family and household cases,
helping to make our homes safer spaces.

The first female Arab-American Muslim judge in the nation,
her well-deserved achievements are an inspiration.

- Journalist
- Performing Artist

Ha Ha Ha

MARIAM SOBH

Mariam Sobh is a talented performer
and she has proved to be no conformer!

She's gifted, indeed,
and will make you laugh, guaranteed!

Making Islam and her hijab of central importance,
she's earned awards and recognitions for her outstanding performance.

Activist

AMANI AL-KHATAHTBEH

Amani Al-Khatahtbeh is one of the most influential American Muslims.
She writes and talks about her heritage and customs.

She shares stories about being a Muslim lady,
and highlights unfair treatment of her community on a daily.

She got involved in politics to try to further change,
and is willing to "talk back" until there's a societal rearrange.

ISRA CHAKER

Isra Chaker is an exceptional speaker.
She is an advocate for the peace seekers.

She voices her opinion on many political panels
and supports refugees on various news channels.

She speaks passionately to Muslim-American youth
about being themselves and living their truth.

AMANDA SAAB

Amanda Saab started baking with her mother when she was a little girl.
Then when she grew up, her life took an unexpected twirl.

She started creating delicious recipes.
Before she knew it, food became her legacy!

The first Muslim woman in hijab on an American cooking competition,
Amanda's cooking has now brought her worldwide recognition.

HALIMA ADEN

Halima Aden is the first Muslim in hijab to be an icon in American fashion.
Embracing her style and cultural pride, she blends both her passions.

Showcased in burkinis on many fashion stages,
she's even struck a pose on magazines' front pages.

Halima always dresses modestly in beauty competitions.
Chic and confident, she honors her cultural traditions.

MELANIE ELTURK

Melanie Elturk is best known for founding Haute Hijab,
a company whose mission is to make hijabs even more fab.

She has also used her experience as a lawyer to fight for social rights.
Certainly, she is talented, passionate and bright.

She is one of the most successful businesswomen known today.
With the creation of Haute Hijab, she's paved her own way!

INTISAR RABB

Intisar Rabb is highly educated, and a courageous leader.
With degrees from top-ranked schools, she's been a long-time reader.

She helps explain Islamic Sharia and U.S. law so it is better understood,
and educates through her courses for the sake of the greater good.

Teaching Legal Studies at Harvard University, a prestigious school,
she models for students how to live by the rules.

HARVARD

LAYLA SHAIKLEY

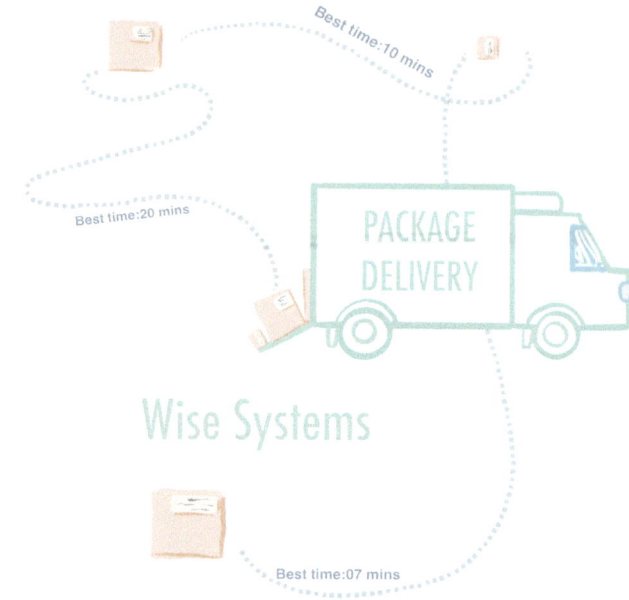

Layla Shaikley is a tech whiz.
Clever and sophisticated, she most definitely is!

She is a computer engineer and trained architect,
and advocates for Muslims to get respect.

Her first startup gathered data and information,
to help improve the quality of people's situations.

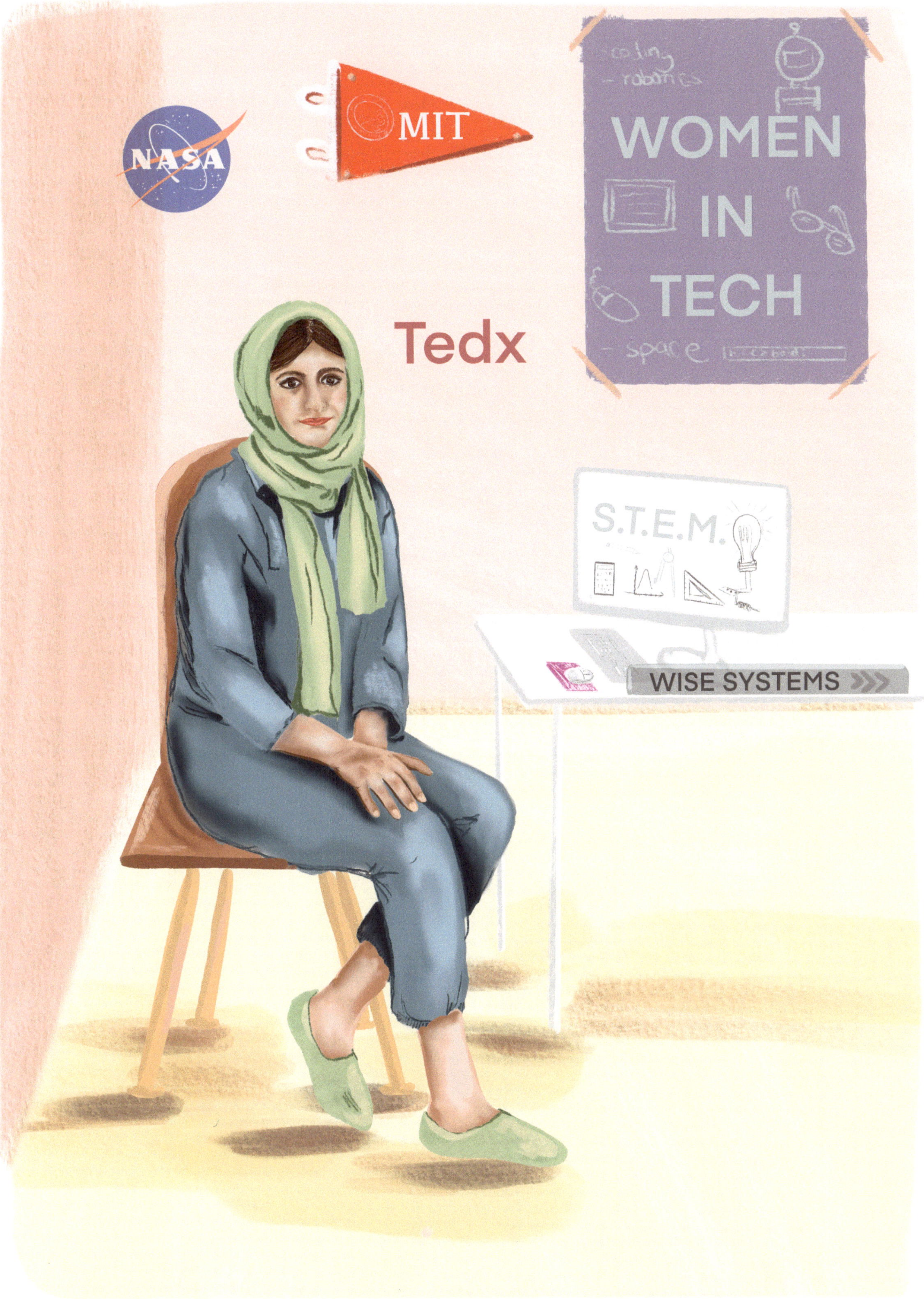
NASA
MIT
WOMEN IN TECH
Tedx
S.T.E.M.
WISE SYSTEMS

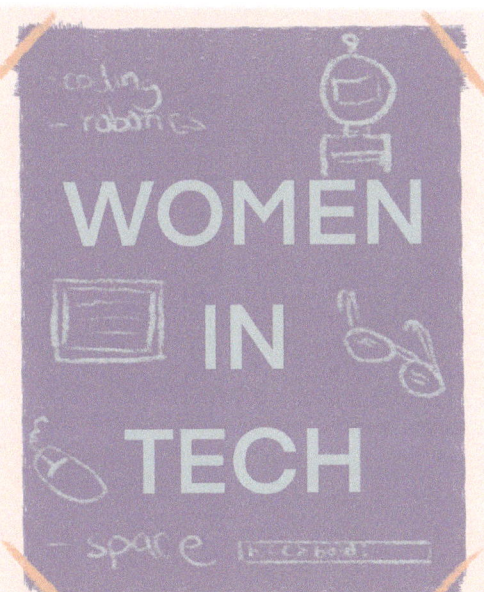

RANIA AWAAD

Rania Awaad is a psychiatrist who teaches at Stanford,
a distinguished school.
She studies mental health,
an important tool.

Her work blends psychology with Islamic lessons,
and helps clients grow through therapy sessions.

Rania researches the needs of Muslims in the United States.
Better mental health is what she aims to create.

Stanford University

SU'AD ABDUL KHABEER

Su'ad Abdul Khabeer teaches Muslim-American studies at university.
An activist with a rich knowledge of social groups,
she embraces diversity.

She educates on culture and religion in schools,
and makes learning hip and cool.

Focusing on Black Muslims,
she always has something inspirational to say.
Su'ad communicates to the world
that we don't all look the same way.

Sapelo Square

DALIA MOGAHED

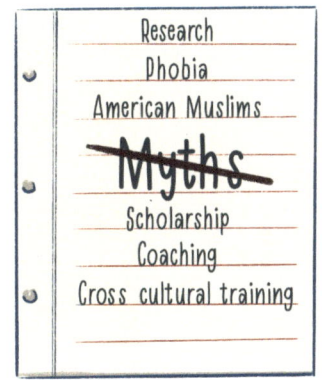

Dalia Mogahed is a researcher, scholar and writer.
She studies Muslim communities for ways to shine brighter.

She explores Muslim identity through different lights,
preventing social problems and working to make things right.

She addresses stereotypes and myths about the Muslim community
and challenges these issues to encourage unity.

AFREEN SIDDIQI

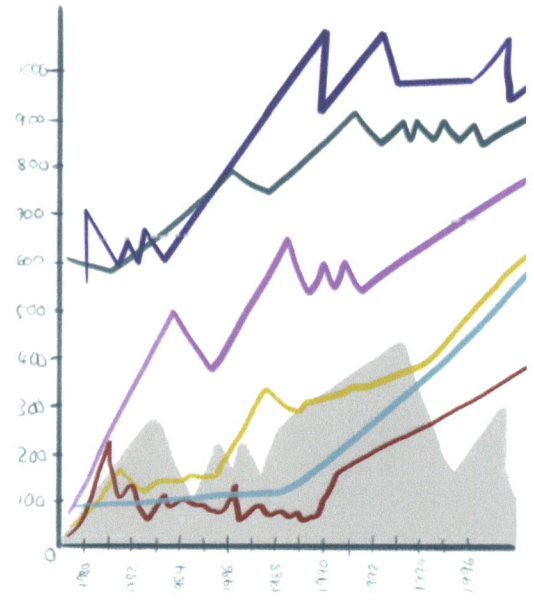

Afreen Siddiqi is an academic engineer with a unique specialization. She focuses her research on scientific education.

Studying water, energy and food, using technology and statistics, her aim is to better utilize resources by improving logistics.

Afreen received awards for her wisdom and skill.
Her talent for mechanical and aerospace engineering
comes from passion and will.

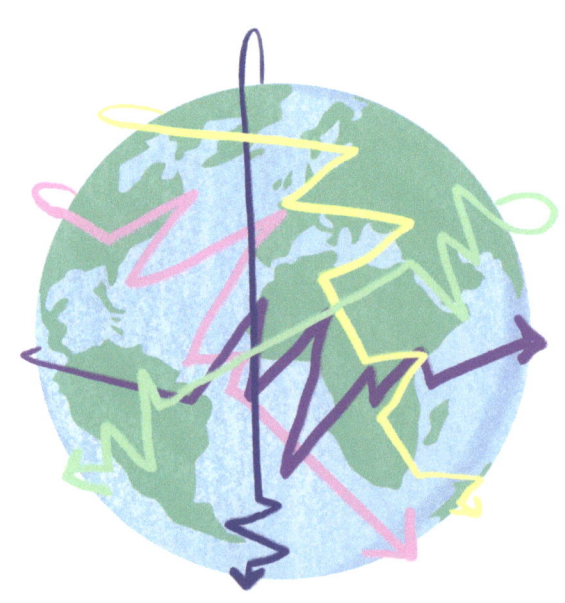

RASHIDA TLAIB

Rashida Tlaib is a politician and attorney.
One of 14 children, she's had an incredible career and journey!

As the first Muslim representing Michigan in Congress,
she's worked hard to make her district the strongest!

Rashida strives to do what's fair for all people in her zone.
Her policies and efforts show her community
that they are not alone.

GWENDOLYN WILLOW WILSON

Gwendolyn Willow Wilson is an author and journalist
with a talent for writing.
Her most famous work is about a Muslim superhero.
How exciting!

She's been recognized for her award-winning stories
and is respected for her work in the comics categories.

Her Muslim characters have various roles
and inspire her readers to fulfill their own goals.

"A *hero* is just somebody who tries to do the *right* thing even when it's hard. There are *more* of us than you think."

G. Willow Wilson

AMANY KILLAWI

Amany Killawi is a business founder who is very influential.
She helps many Muslim causes reach their full potential.

Amany's startup business creates campaigns for people in need,
connecting them with others who can bring them up to speed.

A fundraising platform for emergency support to medical supplies,
Launchgood helps worldwide donations be greater in size.

Discussion Questions

Parents, teachers, and community partners, these questions are crafted for you!

I invite you to initiate dialogue with your children and mentees. Please use these sample questions to provoke thought and have an interactive discussion. I hope you find the content helpful in communicating the importance of being comfortable and confident with who you are, no matter what barriers come your way. I encourage you and your children to share your feedback with me. These women's stories have truly made me proud, and I pray that we continue to shine amidst this ever changing world.

In Peace,
Sara Abdelhadi Bejaoui

Why is it important to recognize notable Muslim women living in America?

What problems do you think these 20 women faced trying to prosper in life?

Do you think the women in this book faced any problems? What would be some examples you can think of?

What do you want to be when you grow up? Did any of these women inspire you to follow in their footsteps?

Do you think growing up Muslim in America is a challenge? How do you think life will change over the next 10 years?

Do these women make you proud? Tell me why.

Who would you like to share this book with? Why do you choose this person or community?

What is something you want to protect, defend, and support in your line of work?

Glossary

Activist	Someone who advocates for and supports an idea, community or cause.
Advocate	Someone who supports an idea or community and works towards the betterment of the cause.
Aerospace	The study of space. Includes studying and producing space ships.
Burkini	A women's swim suit that covers the entire body except the face, hands, and feet.
Campaign	A team with a goal to win something.
Category	A specific section.
Conformer	To agree or support a group and their community standards.
Culture	A shared set of ideas, beliefs, customs, traditions, religion, etc, shared by a large group of people.
Custom	A regular practice that can be shared among a community.
Dedicated	Devoted and committed to.
Devout	Complete commitment and loyalty to.
District	A space or territory that organizes cities/states.
Donation	Giving away money or objects for a good cause.
Doubt	Having uncertainty.; unsure of something.
Embrace	A physical act of hugging or the acceptance of something.
Generation	A family line.
Grudge	Holding a lasting negative view point towards someone or something.
Heritage	Consists of customs, practices, and traditions that has been passed down family generations.
Influential	A source of inspiration. To admire.
Inspiration	The feeling of wanting to do something creative
Legacy	A message, idea, or foundation (material or abstract) left behind to be continued by new generations.
Logistics	The operations and organized procedure.
Mentor	A guide to help advise usually based off of personal experience.
Myth	A story that is not proven to be true.

Nation	A community officially organized through politics, territory, language, culture, etc.
Opportunity	A favorable chance to do something or have something.
Panels	A selected group of experts.
Passion	An extremely strong driving force that can influence inspiration and devotion to something or someone.
Pave	To prepare or create a plan.
Pioneer	Among the first to explore and develop for others to follow.
Policy	A law or recommendation.
Politics	Government based activity that has strong power and influence on its nation.
Potential	Has possibility.
Prestigious	Respected, honorable, highly accredited.
Quality	Having excellent features and characteristics.
Rearrange	To change.
Recognition	Acknowledgment.
Scholar	An intelligent expert in a certain subject.
Seeker	A person in search of or looking for.
Social	Having interaction with others.
Specialization	Having expertise in a certain subject.
Statistics	Facts based on numbers, measurements, collected research and qualitative data.
Stereotype	A fixed idea of someone usually based of religion, race, gender, or ethnicity.
Tradition	Consists of customs and practices that has been passed down family generations.
Unity	Joined force. The act of gathering.
Whiz	A highly skilled or intelligent person.
Will	To be determined.
Wisdom	Higher knowledge usually gained from greater experience and/or age.
Youth	Young people.
Zone	A physical space or region.

Biographies

Mariam Sobh is an award-winning journalist, comedy writer and producer. She is a broadcast news anchor and reporter in Chicago, Illinois. Sobh wrote and performed in a comedy show, "Headscarf Above Water," a story of an American Muslim woman. She has also participated in various other comedy festivals and events. She is now a digital content creator and has created a life blog that emphasizes Muslim women.

Ibtihaj Muhammad is an American Olympic gold medalist. She won bronze at the 2016 Rio Olympic Games becoming the first Muslim-American woman to win an Olympic medal. She is also the first USA athlete to compete at the Olympic games wearing a hijab. Muhammad has been named the 2016 TIME magazine 100 Most Influential People, the 2012 Muslim Sportswoman of the Year, and Nike's pro-hijab ambassador. In 2017, Mattel released the first Barbie doll with a hijab and fencing suit to commemorate Muhammad.

Anousheh Ansari is a breakthrough astronaut, born in Iran in 1966. She earned a BS from George Mason University in electronics and computer engineering, a George Washington University master's degree in electrical engineering, and an honorary doctorate from the International Space University. Ansari is the co-founder of Prodea Systems, the co-founder and CEO of Telecom Technologies, Inc., and the CEO of X Prize Foundation. In 2006, she became the first Iranian Muslim female private astronaut

Noor Tagouri is a Libyan-American award-winning journalist, producer, and activist. She graduated from the University of Maryland with a degree in broadcast journalism. She has produced a modern day docu-series and podcasts depicting marginalized and underserved communities in the US gaining millions of views. In 2016, her podcast docu-series, Sold in America: Inside Our Nation's Sex Trade, received a Best Investigative Series Gracies award. She was the first Muslim woman in hijab to appear in a fully clothed 2016 "Renegades Issue" of Playboy magazine. Tagouri is founder and producer of At Your Service (AYS), a production company.

Since 2005, **Charlene M. Elder** has served as a judge of the Third Circuit Court in Wayne County. Her branch of law is Family Division. Elder developed the Domestic Violence Prevention Court. She graduated from the University of Michigan and earned her juris doctor degree from the Detroit College of Law.

Amani Al-Khatahtbeh is a Jordanian-American author and activist born in 1992. In 2009, she founded a digital startup "Muslim Girl," a space to represent and celebrate Muslim women. She created the first official Muslim Women's Day on MuslimGirl.com. Al-Khatahtbeh has developed a special Getty Images series, which is led, filmed and performed by real and diverse Muslim women. Al-Khatahtbeh was featured on Forbes "30 under 30" list and named one of the 25 most influential Muslim-Americans by CNN. In 2020, Al-Khatahtbeh became the first Muslim woman to run for the representation of New Jersey's 6th in the House of Representatives.

Zarina Ali is a renowned neurosurgeon from Staten Island, New York. She is Pennsylvania Hospital's first female neurosurgeon and is now an Assistant Professor of Neurosurgery at U Penn. Dr. Ali received her PhD from the University of Rochester School of Medicine and Dentistry. She is the founder and director of the Enhanced Recovery After Neurosurgery (ERAS) program in Pennsylvania.

Isra Chaker is a Syrian-American Muslim civil rights activist. She earned a master's degree from George Mason University in Global Affairs and Public Policy. She is now the Refugee, Migration, and Protection Campaign Lead for Oxfam focusing her work on support for refugees and asylum seekers specifically from Syria. Isra has consulted with television and streaming networks including Netflix and ABC on authenticity and accurate portrayal of Muslim and Arab-American characters and narrative. She is an ICON for the "We The Future" campaign by Amplifier. She is the CEO of Chaker Solutions LLC, a leadership training program.

Amanda Saab is a chef, baker, and entrepreneur from Michigan. Saab's master's degree is in social work from Wayne State University. In 2017, she opened an American-Middle Eastern fusion bakery. She is known as the first woman in a Hijab on an American cooking prime time television show (Masterchef on Fox). She has been featured in a series for the Today Show called, "Dinner With Your Muslim Neighbor," and Lifetime docu-series called, "Chef in Hijab." Amanda is currently an opportunity manager in the civil rights department for the City of Detroit. Chef Saab also runs a blog, "Amanda's Plate."

Halima Aden competed in the 2016 Miss Minnesota USA becoming the first contestant to wear a hijab and burkini (she was a semi-finalist). She is known as the first mainstream supermodel to wear a hijab. She was the first model to wear a headscarf and a burkini on the covers of Sports Illustrated and Vogue magazines.

Melanie Elturk is a civil rights attorney and entrepreneur from Detroit, Michigan. She is of Lebanese and Filipino descent. She graduated from Wayne University with a Bachelor of Arts degree in Sociology and English, and later a degree in Law. Before co-founding Haute Hijan, the top American headscarf brand, she was a civil rights lawyer. The brand focuses on sustainability, gives functionality, and provides high performance for high fashion headscarves.

Intisar Rabb is an expert in law. She received a BA and BS from Georgetown University, an MA and PhD from Princeton University, and a JD from Yale Law School. She is program director of Islamic Law for Harvard University as well as a professor of law and history. Dr. Rabb is associate professor at New York University for the Department of Middle Eastern and Islamic Studies. She also served as law clerk for a judge of the United States Court of Appeals. In 2015, she developed SHARIAsource – an online source for Islamic law and history. She has various publications on Islamic law. Rabb was awarded the Trailblazer Awards by Massachusetts Black Lawyers Association in 2018.

Layla Shaikley is an Iraqi-American technology and software expert. She earned her bachelor's degree in art and political science from the University of Irvine, her masters in architecture from California Polytechnic University, and her masters in science in architecture from MIT. In 2010, she started an internship at NASA, where she designed the robot. Later, she co-founded a software startup company called Wise Systems. In 2010, Shaikley co-founded TEDxBaghdad, a platform for Iraqi innovations.

Rania Awaad is an Egyptian advocate for the mental health of women, refugees, and Muslims. She serves as director and assistant professor for Stanford University as well as a psychiatrist at Stanford University's School of Medicine. Dr. Awaad has worked overseas to support Syrian and Iraqi refugees. She is also a professor of Islamic law at Zaytuna College in California. Dr. Awaad has been awarded the Arnold P. Gold Foundation Award for Humanism and Excellence in Teaching and has published various research findings.

Amany Killawi is a social worker, entrepreneur and political activist based in Virginia. She graduated from Wayne State University in 2013 with a degree in social work. She co-founded the Detroit Minds and Hearts Fellowship, a program to support inner city Muslim youth. In 2013, she co-founded LaunchGood.com, a platform supporting projects by Muslims all over the world, and is now the company's COO. Killawi was named Inc. Magazine's 2020 Top 100 Female Founders in the community builders' category.

Su'ad Abdul Khabeer is a scholarly activist. In 2011, she earned her Ph.D. in cultural anthropology from Princeton University. She is now an Associate Professor of American Culture and Arab and Muslim American Studies at the University of Michigan and has also taught at Purdue University and Loyola University, Chicago. Abdul Khabeer's book, "Muslim Cool: Race, Religion and Hip Hop in the United States," and performance, "Sampled: Beats of Muslim Life," showcase the Black Muslim American experience. In 2018, Su'ad was named "Top 25 influential American Muslims" by CNN. She is the founder and senior editor of Sapelo Square.

Gwendolyn Willow Wilson is a distinguished author born in 1982 in New Jersey. In 2014, she co-created "Ms. Marvel," an award-winning Marvel comic featuring a Pakistani-American Muslim superhero – first Muslim Marvel character with its own series. Wilson has also contributed to other historical superhero comic book series including: "The X-Men," "Superman," and "Wonderwoman."

Rashida Tlaib is a Palestinian-American Democratic politician. In 2008, Tlaib became the first Muslim woman to serve in the Michigan Legislature for the US House of Representatives. In 2019, she was elected as a Congresswoman for Michigan becoming the first Palestinian-American woman to be elected to Congress.

Afreen Siddiqi is a research scientist and STEM professional. She holds a bachelor's degree in mechanical engineering from the Massachusetts Institute of Technology, a master of science in aerospace science and a doctorate in aerospace systems. Dr. Siddiqi is an Associate Director of the MIT Strategic Engineering Research Group. She is currently working on projects with NASA's space exploration teams. She has over 85 research publications on technology and international policy. Dr. Siddiqi has received the Amelia Earhart Fellowship, Richard D. DuPont Fellowship, and the Rene H. Miller Prize.

Dalia Mogahed is the Director of Research at the Institute for Social Policy and Understanding, where she focuses on developing opportunities for Muslims in the US. Dalia held the role as a member of President Obama's Advisory Council on Faith-Based and Neighborhood Partnerships. Her 2016 TED talk, "What it's like to be Muslim in America," was one of the most watched TED talks of 2016. She is the CEO of Mogahed Consulting, a consulting firm with and for Muslims. In 2018, she was named "the 25 Most Influential Muslim Americans" by CNN.

Bibliography

https://mariamsobh.com/about/

https://www.ibtihajmuhammad.com/

https://www.xprize.org/about/people/anousheh-ansari

https://www.noortagouri.com/

https://ballotpedia.org/Charlene_Elder

https://www.cnn.com/interactive/2018/05/us/influential-muslims/#al-khatahtbeh

https://www.oyeyeah.com/blogs/zarina-ali-penn-hospitals-first-muslim-female-neurosurgeon/

https://www.israspeaks.com/

https://www.eater.com/2015/5/21/8640161/masterchefs-amanda-saab-is-the-first-woman-in-a-hijab-on-an-american

https://pagesix.com/2020/07/22/halima-aden-sports-illustrateds-first-burkini-wearing-model-is-back/

https://www.hautehijab.com/blogs/hijab-fashion/15-things-you-may-not-know-about-hhs-melanie-elturk-ceo

https://hls.harvard.edu/faculty/directory/11205/Rabb

https://money.cnn.com/interactive/technology/15-questions-with-layla-shaikley/index.html

https://profiles.stanford.edu/Rania_Awaad

http://www.suadabdulkhabeer.com/

https://www.ispu.org/dalia-mogahed/

https://www.hks.harvard.edu/faculty/afreen-siddiqi

https://tlaib.house.gov/

https://www.gwillowwilson.com/

https://www.tech-sisters.com/2019/11/my-life-as-a-startup-founder-interview-with-amany-killawi/

www.ingramcontent.com/pod-product-compliance
Lightning Source LLC
Chambersburg PA
CBHW041716160426
43209CB00018B/1847